LEVEL THREE (ADVANCED INTERMEDIATE)

Studies and Melodious Etudes for Clarinet

by
Robert Lowry
in collaboration with
James Ployhar

To The Teacher

"Studies And Melodious Etudes", Level III, is a supplementary technic book of the Belwin "STUDENT INSTRUMENTAL COURSE". Although planned as a companion and correlating book to the method, "The Clarinet Student", it can also be used effectively with most intermediate or advanced clarinet instruction books. It provides for extended and additional treatment in technical areas, which are limited in the basic method because of lack of space. Emphasis is on developing musicianship through scales, warm-ups and technical drills, musicianship studies and interesting melody-like etudes.

The Belwin "STUDENT INSTRUMENTAL COURSE" - A course for individual and class instruction of LIKE instruments, at three levels, for all band instruments.

EACH BOOK IS COMPLETE IN ITSELF BUT ALL BOOKS ARE CORRELATED WITH EACH OTHER

METHOD
"The B♭ Clarinet Student"
For Individual or Clarinet Class Instruction.

ALTHOUGH EACH BOOK CAN BE USED SEPARATELY, IDEALLY, ALL SUPPLEMENTARY BOOKS SHOULD BE USED AS COMPANION BOOKS WITH THE METHOD

STUDIES & MELODIOUS ETUDES
Supplementary scales, warm-up and technical drills, musicianship studies and melody-like etudes, all carefully correlated with the method.

TUNES FOR TECHNIC
Technical type melodies, variations, and "famous passages" from musical literature for the development of technical dexterity.

B♭ CLARINET SOLOS
Four separate correlated Solos, with piano accompaniment, selected, written or arranged by Robert Lowry:
A Festival Fantasie .... *Lowry*
Prelude .... *Jarnefelt*
Melody .... *Paderewski*
Lucia di Lammermoor
.... *Donizetti*

CLARINET FINGERING CHART

How To Read The Chart

● Indicates hole closed, or keys to be pressed.   ○ Indicates hole open.

When a numer is given, refer to the picture of the Clarinet for additional key to be pressed.

When two notes are given together (ex: F♯ and G♭), they are the same tone (enharmonic) and, of course, played the same way.

When there are two or more fingerings for a note, use the first one notated unless your teacher tells you or the music dictates otherwise.

CHART CODE

- **Chr.** Indicates that this fingering is the smoothest and best in a chromatic passage.
- **F** A "false fingering" indicating that the tone quality or intonation may be a bit faulty. It will, however, be useful in a very rapid passage when a smooth technic becomes more important than absolutely perfect pitch.
- **Tr.** This designates a fingering that may be a bit false, but will be very practical for trills.
- **R or L** Tells you which "Right or Left" little finger is involved for the particular fingering.
- **RHD** The abbreviation for "Right Hand (fingers) Down". This will add more resonance to your tone in the throat register and simplify technic over the register break.
- **1/1** The common abbreviation for low E♭ or high B♭ when the first finger of each hand (plus the left thumb) is to be used.

© 1971 (Renewed) BELWIN-MILLS PUBLISHING CORP.
All Rights Assigned to and Controlled by ALFRED MUSIC PUBLISHING CO., INC.
All Rights Reserved.   Printed in USA.

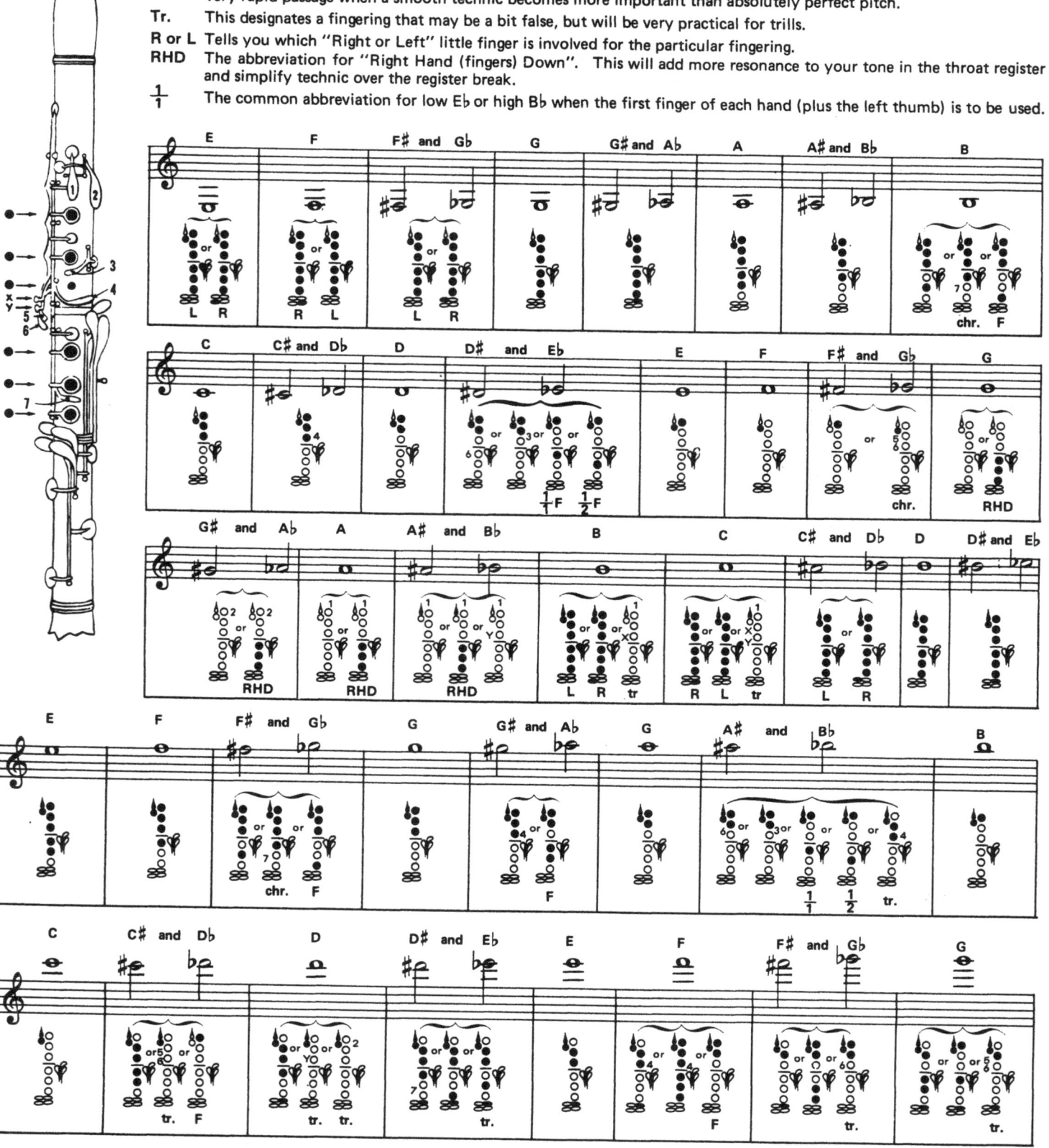

The Studies and Etudes on this page approximately correlate with Page 8 of the B♭ Clarinet method book "The Clarinet Student", Level III, and the correlation is continued throughout the book.

C Major Studies

Slowly and smoothly

Make the wide interval skips with the register key by merely bending the left thumb knuckle.

Moderato

Chromatics - In four.

*F♭ - Enharmonic to (same as) E♮.

In an easy two.

Etude No. 1

HYACINTHE KLOSE

D. S. al Fine

© 1971 (Renewed) BELWIN-MILLS PUBLISHING CORP.
All Rights Assigned to and Controlled by ALFRED MUSIC PUBLISHING CO., INC.
All Rights Reserved. Printed in USA.

Syncopation

Watch the rhythm

Etude No. 2

*Remember to use the better chromatic fingerings.

same as C↓   same as D↓
same as F↓   same as G↓

Etude No. 3

HENRY LAZARUS

Etude No. 4

Please see the book "TUNES FOR CLARINET TECHNIC", Level III, for more melodies that provide for further technical development.

The register key should be opened by a mere bend of the thumb knuckle.

Etude No. 5

CARL BAERMANN

Use the top two side keys for the B♭ to C trills.

reg.

For dynamic extremes.

Use the B♭ to C trill fingering for speed.

Etude No. 6

Majestically

Play the staccato notes lightly.

Etude No. 7

GUSTAVE LANGENUS

Etude No. 8

Vivace in three.

Review the list of correlated solos listed at the top of page 13. These interesting solos were written specifically for this course and will enhance the study of your instrument. We suggest that you supplement your lesson assignments with one of these solos at all times.

Etude No. 9

H. KLOSE

Etude No. 10

Moderato in two.

Solo listing:	A Festival Fantasia — *Robert Lowry*
	Prelude — *Armas Jarnefelt*
	Melody — *Ignace Jan Paderewski*
	Lucia di Lammermoor — *Gaelano Donizetti*

Andante (in one)
Low tone study

Syncopation in D Major

Etude No. 11

Tempo di Valse

HENRY LAZARUS

Etude No. 12

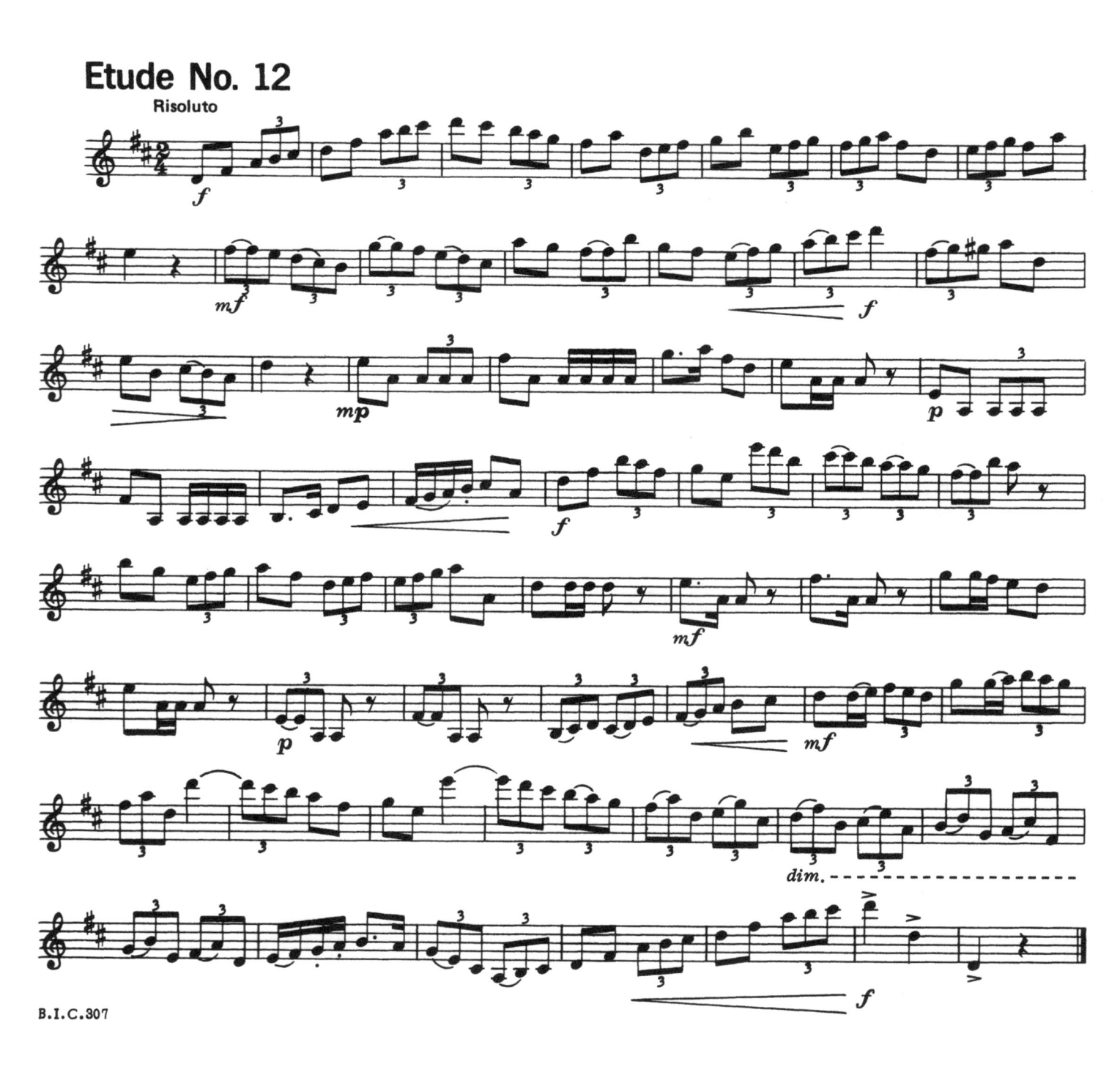

Etude No. 13

ABBATE BERTINI

Allegretto in D minor

Watch the articulations.

High note study

Staccato Study

JACQUES MAZAS

Keep it light - Don't accent.

Etude No. 14

Allegro moderato

March tempo

side B♭

Study in C minor.

Etude No. 15

H. KLOSE

Allegretto

smoothly

Fine

sim.

cresc.

Cadenza

start slowly — — — accel. — — — — rit.

D. S. al Fine

Etude No. 16

In four

Major arpeggios in chromatic sequence.

In one

Etude No. 17
Allegro non troppo

FRANZ BERR

Etude No. 18

*Use top two side keys for trill.

Watch the syncopated measures closely.

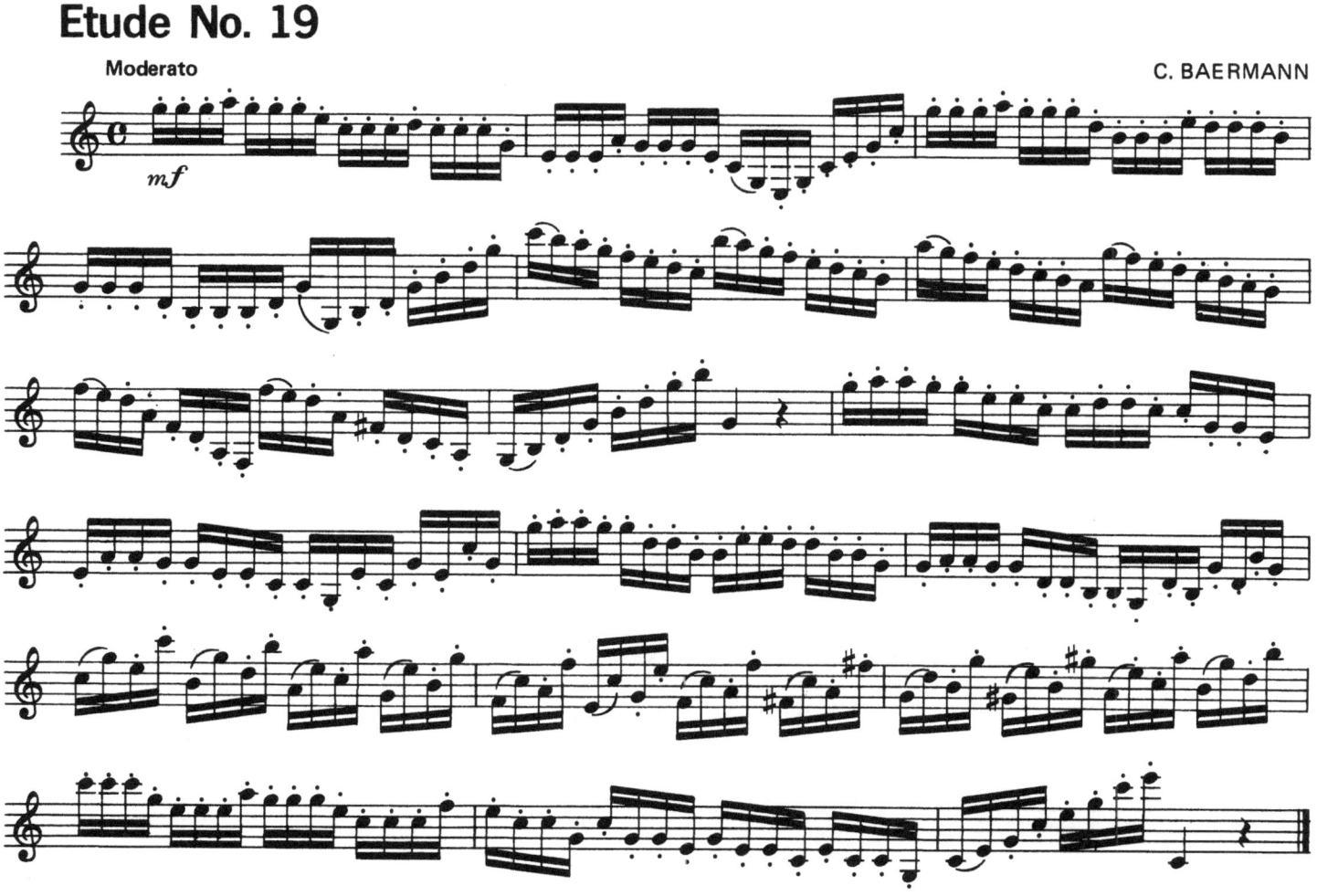

Etude No. 19

Moderato
C. BAERMANN

Etude No. 22

*Refer to page 28 for drill on this awkward fingering problem.

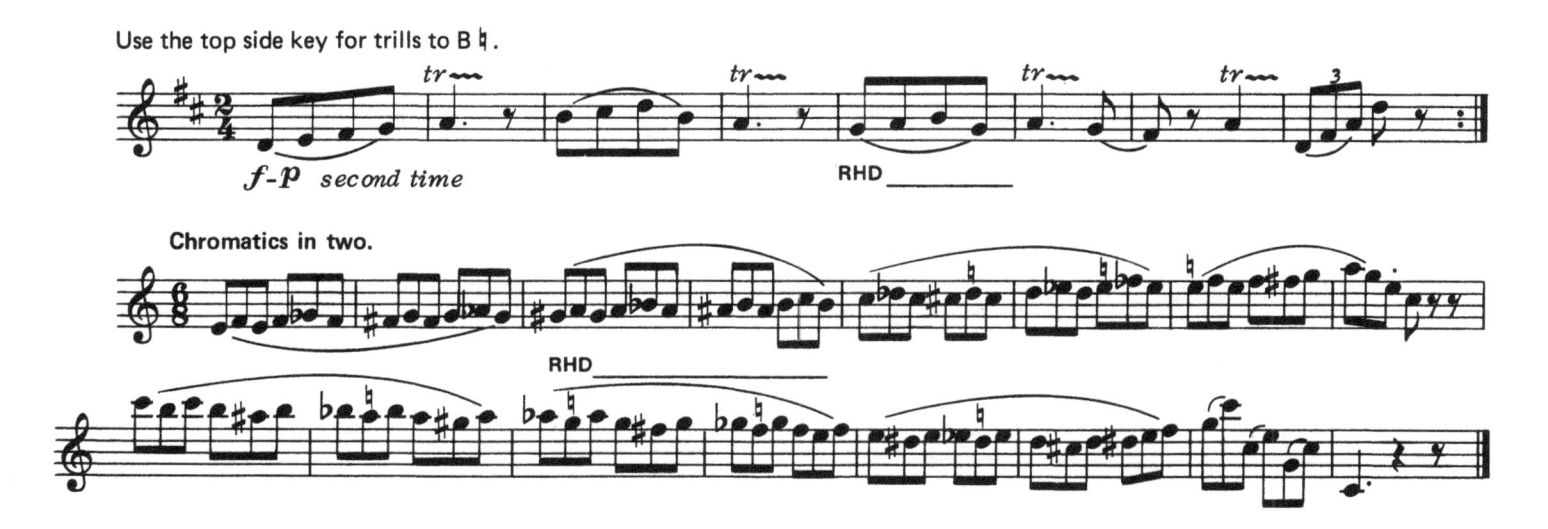

Use the top side key for trills to B♮.

f-p second time

Chromatics in two.

Etude No. 21

Allegro in F# minor

A. BERTINI

rit. e dim. , *a tempo*

Larghetto

Major arpeggios in chromatic sequence

Etude No. 22

Look for the many places whereby leaving your right hand fingers down simplifies smoothness over the register break.

Allegro (in two)

Etude No. 23

J. MAZAS

Chromatics

This study treats one of the most awkward finger patterns on the plain boehm system clarinet.

Keep the fingering between C♯ and D♯ clean at all times.

Etude No. 24

Speed Study

C# minor

Etude No. 25

Allegretto

LUDWIG SPOHR

Intervals in G♭ Major

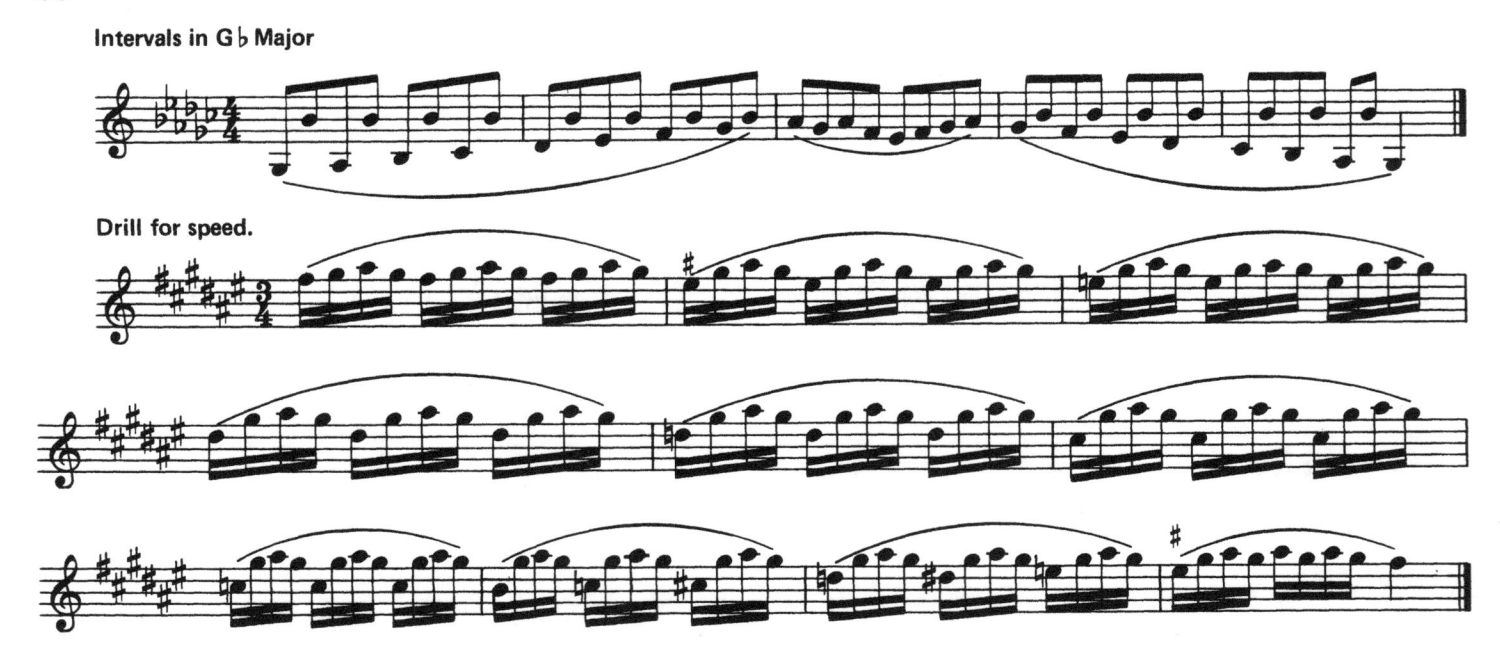

Drill for speed.

Etude No. 26

Andante

Although the situation does not occur often there are times when certain passages cannot be smoothly alternated between the right and left little finger keys.

This problem can be solved by employing one of the three following methods.

1. In slow passages, use a "silent exchange". Shift from R to L (or L to R) while holding the same note. See example ❶
2. For rapid passages, "glide" from a key to another key with the same little finger. It is best to plan these "glides" in a downward motion. See example ❷
3. Even though a passage may be under a slur, in some circumstances it is smoother to legato tongue lightly allowing the little finger time to reach for another key. Example ❸

Etude No. 27

C. ROSE

Major and Relative Minor Scales

Memorize and practice these scales using the following articulation patterns.

B♭ minor
G♭ Major
E♭ minor
B Major
G♯ minor
E Major
C♯ minor
A Major
F♯ minor
D Major
B minor
G Major
E minor
C Major

Classified Intervals

All music ever composed is simply various scales and arpeggios put together in different rhythm patterns. Towards improving your sight reading ability, it is therefore wise to memorize and develop a reflex finger pattern for all of the following intervals.

Chromatic Scale (Half steps)

Practice all of these studies with various articulation patterns of your choice.

Whole tone Scales (Whole steps)

Diminished Seventh Arpeggios (Minor thirds)

Augmented arpeggios (Major thirds)

B.I.C.307